The Peace Seekers

The Peace Seekers

The Nobel Peace Prize

by Nathan Aaseng

Lerner Publications Company • Minneapolis

To Scott and Gale

This book is available in two editions:
Library binding by Lerner Publications Company
Soft cover by First Avenue Editions
241 First Avenue North
Minneapolis, Minnesota 55401

The glossary on page 76 gives definitions for the words
in bold face type.

Excerpt from "I Have a Dream" by Martin Luther
King, Jr., reprinted by permission of Joan Daves.
Copyright © 1963 by Martin Luther King, Jr.

LIBRARY OF CONGRESS CATALOGING-IN-PUBLICATION DATA

Aaseng, Nathan.
    The peace seekers.

    (Nobel Prize winners)
    Includes index.
    Summary: Profiles of nine Nobel Peace Prize winners
who fought for peace by resisting violence through
words, marches, and protests.
    1. Pacifists—Biography—Juvenile literature.
2. Nobel prizes—Juvenile literature. 3. Peace—
Juvenile literature. [1. Pacifists. 2. Nobel prizes.]
I. Title. II. Series.
JX1962.A2A18   1987   327.1′72′0922   [B] [920]   87-4257
ISBN 0-8225-0654-8 (lib. bdg.)
ISBN 0-8225-9604-0 (pbk.)

Manufactured in the United States of America

    4   5   6   7   8   9   10   96   95   94   93   92

Contents

Martin Luther King, Jr., is congratulated by King Olav V of Norway after receiving the 1964 Nobel Peace Prize.

Introduction

If you were expecting a book about gentle people who are loved and admired by everyone because of their noble natures, then you've come to the wrong place. Prepare instead to meet individuals who have been publicly described as "the most dangerous woman," "the most notorious liar," and "the most shameless traitor" and have been called far worse names in private.

Prepare to meet people who once received one of the world's highest honors, only to have the award of that honor denounced as an "insult" by officials in countries as diverse as the United States and the Soviet Union. As if that weren't enough, consider that this special prize was financed by a man whose invention has blown apart billions of dollars of property and killed untold millions of people.

In exactly what terrible activity have these people been engaged that has brought them such scorn and hatred that they have been slandered, physically attacked, jailed, even tortured and killed?

The answer: peace.

What we have before us is a puzzle that is far more difficult than any brainteaser ever devised. We live in a world in which peace is at the top of nearly everyone's wish list, yet the most venomous hatred is poured out on some of those who threaten to make that dream a reality. Peace is an elusive goal, and its pursuit can be the ultimate frustration.

The Nobel Peace Prize was born out of frustration. Alfred Nobel, the Swedish scientist who invented dynamite, once expressed the hope that his terrible new explosives would force the world to abandon warfare forever. Dynamite seemed to him to be such an awesome killing force that no one would dare use it as a weapon. Although he did not live to see the world wars that reduced his theory to ashes, Nobel came to understand that peace through horror had no hope of surviving and that dreadful wars were inevitable. His inventions had not made mass killings impossible, they had made them easier.

Nations were willing to pay handsomely for the power to destroy life in large doses, and Alfred Nobel became a very rich man. At the end of his life, the conscience-stricken Nobel sought to salvage what he could out of the situation by using the money he had earned from dynamite to promote life, not destroy it. His will stated that the profits from the investment of that money would be used to fund five annual awards. Four of the awards were to be given to the people who had contributed the most in the areas of chemistry, physics, physiology or medicine, and literature during the previous year. The fifth, the Nobel Peace Prize, would be awarded to the person or persons who had most advanced the cause of peace.

The Challenge of Peace

Many kinds of people have won the Nobel Peace Prize and for many different reasons. It doesn't matter where they are from—the United States, Poland, Ireland, South Africa, Germany, or the Soviet Union—or what they do for a living. The flame of conscience can burn as brightly in a social reformer as in an electrician, in a preacher as in a scientist, in an archbishop as in a homemaker.

The nine people described in this book were chosen because they best illustrate

Swedish chemist Alfred Nobel established the Nobel Prizes.

the irony that peace cannot be wished on the world; it must be fought for. These were the fighters who believed in making noise and challenging widely accepted beliefs. Rather than smoothing ruffled feathers, they stood up to the enemies of peace and attacked them with words, marches, and protests. When these committed men and women were frustrated with the action or inaction of governments that stood in the way of their goals, they dared to oppose them. When waves of public opinion turned against them, they struggled on alone.

Have these people really accomplished anything or is the Nobel Peace Prize just a pat on the back for good intentions? At times, some efforts seem to be only temporary triumphs; it is not until years after an effort has begun, like Lech Walesa's Solidarity movement in Poland, that change occurs. Other efforts have more immediate results, such as Linus Pauling's test ban treaty and Martin Luther King, Jr.'s fight to improve the status of minorities. But even the most effective of the Nobel Prize winners has taken us only a tiny distance on the road to peace. There is still discrimination in the United States and in South Africa.

There are also far more nuclear weapons ready for action now than when Pauling was warning of their dangers, in spite of worldwide efforts to lessen this number.

What has been the result of Nobel's peace award? Frustration and more frustration. The recipients of the Nobel Peace Prize realize what they are up against, yet they continue to fight for peace because they see no other choice. They know that peace cannot come about without change, and change never happens without the agonizing sacrifice of the old. Their efforts are not perfect, their methods sometimes debatable, and their successes far too few; but the stories of their protests and challenges live on to influence others to keep at the monumental task and to hold on to the hope for a better world.

The Nobel medal for peace. On the front (left) is a bust of Alfred Nobel, and on the back (right) is an engraving that represents the bonds of brotherhood.

1

Jane Addams versus the Great Adventure

At the dawn of the 20th century, there was intense competition for power among European nations. Spending heavily to stockpile weapons, the countries took pride in honing their military skills to a fine edge. Threats of war were given and taken without alarm; such threats were the accepted method of conducting **diplomacy.** They were like carefree youngsters canoeing on a river, too wrapped up in the excitement of their progress to notice that the current was pulling them toward a deadly waterfall. Eventually, the threats had to be backed up with actions in order to be taken seriously.

Jane Addams (right) carried the banner for peace during a time when it was a very unpopular cause.

Even when war was finally declared in 1914, many people reacted with excitement, rather than with fear or shock. Historians speak of the romantic joy that accompanied the start of the war that would come to be called World War I. There was a feeling that this was a great adventure—a chance to show the world just what your country could do. People on both sides felt that their military represented the highest values of civilized society at that time: discipline, manliness, patriotism, and justice.

The pro-war sentiment was so strong that those who wanted to voice a different view did so at their own risk. Jane Addams was a prime example of the high price that is often paid by those who seek peace. For many years, Addams was one of the most admired women in the world

11

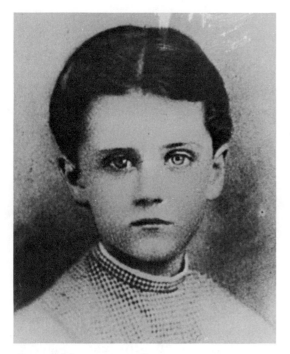

Jane Addams at age 6

because of her selfless dedication to social work. She was never afraid to stand up for the causes she believed in. Ironically, the trait that had won Addams such popularity eventually toppled her from her pedestal when she dared to speak out against the war.

Although Addams was only two when her mother died in 1862, she had a very happy childhood growing up in a prosperous, highly educated midwestern family. Addams never married nor had a family of her own. After a heartbreaking look at the condition of the poor in London and an introduction to the efforts at reform being made in England, Jane Addams adopted humanity as her family.

In 1889, at the age of 29, Addams started the Hull House, an organization that brought culture, friendship, pride, and many social and civic opportunities to thousands of poor immigrants in Chicago. She also worked tirelessly for such social reforms as a child labor law, eight-hour workdays for women, and the first juvenile courts. Addams shied away from nothing in her efforts at bettering lives; although refined and gentle by nature, she even accepted a post as the garbage inspector of Chicago's 19th Ward.

The world-famous Hull House won Addams great admiration, and she was considered by many people to be the ideal of what a woman should be. Her combination of generosity, independence, ability, and gentleness brought her universal respect. But it was not Addams's impressive social work that earned her the Nobel Peace Prize. The prize was a reward for her struggle against the forces that caused and prolonged World War I.

Women's Role in Peace

It was only natural that Addams would become an active member of peace organizations; she believed her mission in life was to bring peace through the nurturing of human life. In her book *Newer Ideals of Peace,* which was published in 1907, Addams described the special role women must take in this task. She believed women had a nurturing instinct that gave them the ability and responsibility to preserve peace. Peace, she said, could be achieved by eliminating want in the world and by helping people to grow and ensuring their freedom.

It didn't take long after the start of World War I for many Europeans to realize that war wasn't as glorious as they had thought it would be. With the advances in weaponry, the war was nothing more than brutal, mindless slaughter, as hundreds of thousands of young men were sacrificed in futile efforts to gain a few miles of enemy soil. In Europe, small groups of people—mostly women—organized to try to end the killing. When they were unable to reason with their own leaders, they turned to the United States in hopes that someone in this influential country, which had not yet entered the war, could put pressure on the Europeans to stop fighting.

Jane Addams and other women who supported peace responded to the Europeans' requests by calling a conference of women's organizations from all over the United States to meet in Washington, D.C., on January 10, 1915. The 3,000 women

Addams established the Hull House (pictured here in 1915) in a bleak section of Chicago.

who gathered in Washington formed a national organization they called the Women's Peace Party, and they named Jane Addams their chairperson. Some of their suggestions for working out a peaceful solution to the chaos in Europe seemed to be patterned after Jane Addams herself. They called for patience, hard work, and understanding to set up a form of continuous **mediation** to end the war. Economics, they said, was a more effective form of diplomacy than guns, and their suggestion of **economic sanctions** against warlike nations has since become a policy accepted worldwide. The Women's Peace Party also called for the removal of the economic causes of war and for the education of young people in the ideals of peace.

Addams then crossed the Atlantic to meet with European peace leaders. The result of their meetings was a decision to carry their peace resolutions to the heads of both neutral and warring nations.

Addams (front, second from left) and other members of the Peace Party pose with the banner that flew from the mast of the ship that took them to the peace conference in Europe in 1915.

Jane Addams was considered to be an ideal example of womanhood before she got involved with the peace movement.

Addams was not very enthusiastic about this plan. Her practical nature told her there was almost no chance that the meetings would do any good, but she agreed that the effort must be made. Although many of the government leaders were sympathetic and appreciative of the women's efforts, none of them would do anything to help. Each was hesitant to call for any negotiation for fear of appearing to be weak.

When Addams returned from Europe, she turned her attention to the United States. After many postponements, her polite but persistent requests to meet with President Woodrow Wilson were finally honored. Addams argued that the United States should take a leadership role in a conference of neutral nations that would help steer Europe toward peace. Wilson was impressed with her presentation but ignored her advice. The United States, like the European countries, did not want to appear weak. The president's advisors were afraid that if the United States undertook a peace role and failed, it would lose its worldwide influence. Addams was deeply hurt when the United States not only refused to get involved in peace negotiations, but also joined in the fighting in 1917.

From Saint to Traitor

At this point, Addams could have retired from the fight for peace in graceful defeat. Although there were some who found her participation in the petitioning of European heads of state to be naive, her reputation was basically still intact. She was just one of many Americans who had opposed entering the war. Once the decision had been made to fight, however, the U.S. government appealed to the patriotism of its citizens and succeeded in convincing them to forget their differences and pull together in support of the

15

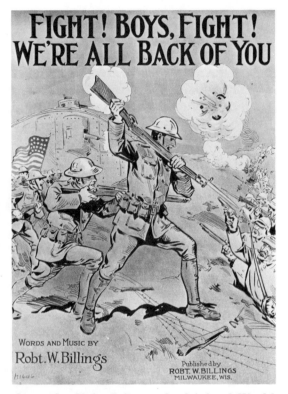

FIGHT! BOYS, FIGHT!
WE'RE ALL BACK OF YOU

WORDS AND MUSIC BY
Robt. W. Billings

Published by
ROBT. W. BILLINGS
MILWAUKEE, WIS.

Once the United States had joined World War I, those who did not rally to songs such as this one were considered to be traitors.

war effort. But Addams, who had always been an expert compromiser, refused to compromise this time.

Jane Addams believed that fighting was wrong, and she especially challenged the idea that war was a glorious and patriotic event. There had to be a better way to show love for your country than dying in a trench. The more she spoke out, saying such things as "soldiers don't like war," the more furious the attacks on her

became. Ex-president Theodore Roosevelt, himself a recipient of the Nobel Peace Prize and a onetime friend of Addams, called her a "silly, vain old maid." Editorials in newspapers throughout the country were even less kind.

Suddenly, the woman who had been called "the greatest American who ever lived" found herself with few friends and virtually no support. A few years before, speakers could guarantee themselves a burst of applause just by mentioning her name; now the name Jane Addams received a chorus of boos. Once organizations had been proud to be associated with Addams; now the Daughters of the American Revolution expelled her from their ranks. Hate mail streamed into her house and angry politicians called her an enemy of the country. After the 1917 Communist Revolution in Russia made people fear Communism, Addams was often whispered to be a Communist supporter. Her name became a symbol for those who wanted to see the United States government overthrown.

Even a person as determined as Jane Addams could barely survive such an assault. She once commented that it seemed almost impossible to hang on to her beliefs against the wave of public opinion. Fortunately, she found an outlet for her energies that would help the government and the cause of peace at the same time. She joined Herbert Hoover's U.S. Food Administration in sending food and other essentials to the devastated people of the warring nations. When the war ended in 1918, Addams urged international cooperation to prevent mass starvation in Europe. That was fine with most Americans until she included the enemy, the Germans, in her efforts. After Addams had spent two years raising money to provide food for hungry German children and then had warned of faults in the Treaty of Versailles—the agreement signed by Germany at the end of the war—she was called a traitor and "the most dangerous woman" in the country.

Consequences of War

The consequences of ignoring Jane Addams and people like her were devastating. Four years of fighting killed 8.5 million soldiers, caused 37.5 million total casualties, and accomplished nothing. At the Battle of Somme alone, the French and English forces advanced approximately seven miles at a cost of more than a half million casualties. The suffering caused by this war did not end in 1918; the problems that Addams foresaw in the Versailles treaty helped to lay the groundwork for an even bigger and more terrible war 20 years later.

Jane Addams continued to serve the cause of peace as president of the Women's International League for Peace and Freedom until 1929. Although nominated for the Nobel Peace Prize as early as 1920, that honor was denied to her for more

It wasn't until late in her life that Addams's efforts to promote peace were recognized.

than a decade. Only gradually did a recognition of the massive contributions and noble character of this dishonored social worker surface from beneath the suspicion. Four years before her death, Addams's efforts to spread her doctrine of peace were finally recognized with the awarding of the 1931 Nobel Peace Prize.

17

2

Carl von Ossietzky
versus a Nation Gone Mad

People who work for peace hold on to the hope that even the cruelest and most corrupt leader has a conscience that can be appealed to by voices of reason. Carl von Ossietzky was denied even that hope in his dealings with Nazi Germany, whose government's vile policies had reached the point of madness in the early 1930s. At the time, many felt that Ossietzky himself must be insane to stand alone against the terrible power of Nazi **terrorism**. If, under the ruthless leadership of Adolf Hitler, the Nazis could murder innocent people by the millions without conscience, then what would they do to

A crowd of Germans join Adolf Hitler (seventh from left) in saluting the swastika, the symbol of the Nazi party.

one lone man who dared to stand up and challenge them?

The seeds of Adolf Hitler's rise to power were sown in the great "war to end all wars" that Jane Addams had tried to stop. Only a few years after the fighting had ended, it became obvious that people had learned nothing from the destruction of World War I. The harsh punishment imposed on Germany by the Treaty of Versailles failed to discourage that country from future military ventures. The majority of Germans did not believe that their army had been defeated and felt that their government should not have accepted the terms of the unfair treaty. Feelings of bitterness and betrayal made them forget the suffering of war, and scarcely had all the dead been buried before **militarism** was on the rise again.

19

Humiliated Germans, who wanted revenge, longed for a restoration of their well-disciplined, powerful army.

The war made a different impression on Carl von Ossietzky, who had fought for Germany in World War I. Always suspicious of the military, he had been fined in 1914 for writing an article criticizing a court decision that went in favor of the army. When Ossietzky was called from his desk job into the infantry, he was appalled by the slaughter he witnessed. He could see nothing heroic about turning young men into piles of dead bodies. As soon as the war was over, Carl von Ossietzky joined the German Peace Society.

A Menace to the State

An intense, uncompromising individual, Ossietzky had little patience with the niceties of politics, and he soon tired of doing office work for the Peace Society. He decided to use his writing skill to wage his own personal campaign for peace. After writing for various papers, Ossietzky joined a magazine called *Die Weltbuhne (The World Stage)*. He moved up to the position of editor in 1926, which gave him the power to determine what the magazine would print. *Die Weltbuhne,* which was known as the conscience of the German republic, tried to persuade people to abandon their militaristic attitudes in favor of peace.

Carl von Ossietzky

Ossietzky shattered the image of a pacifist as a meek, docile individual who dislikes any kind of conflict. Instead of seeking peace through gentle persuasion, he was out to do battle with those who advocated violence. The journalist publicly cursed meek do-gooders and the "spineless" government heads who were trying to direct the country without offending anyone. He scoffed at those who restricted their protests against war to a refusal to bear arms, which in his mind did no good. Ossietzky used his pen to aggressively attack those who favored violence. He sought out groups or individuals who secretly planned for war and exposed them so that they could not hide behind lies and ambiguous statements of policy. One of his most unpopular ways of doing this was to report on the secret **rearmament** being carried out by the government.

According to the terms of the Versailles treaty, Germany was to limit its army to 100,000 soldiers, and it could keep no offensive weapons. Even under the moderate leadership of the shaky Weimar republic, which governed Germany after World War I, secret plans were being carried out to get around these and other provisions of the treaty. Ossietzky agreed with his fellow Germans that the Versailles treaty was unfair and unworkable, but he advocated open negotiations to modify the treaty and correct its faults rather than resort once again to armed conflict.

From the time he took over at *Die Weltbuhne,* Ossietzky was constantly in trouble with the German government, which considered him to be a menace to the state because of his fearless expression of his controversial opinions. He first drew an angry response when he printed an article that criticized government authorities for protecting military leaders from prosecution. Then in 1927 an article that appeared in *Die Weltbuhne* accused the government of condoning **paramilitary organizations** made up of uniformed thugs who were used to intimidate political opponents. Although he spent a month in prison for publishing the article, Ossietzky continued to criticize Germany's government.

No Hope for Survival

Two years after Ossietzky's prison term, his magazine printed an article that exposed a host of secret military activities undertaken by the German government. The article, written by an aircraft technician, revealed that German pilots were being trained at Soviet airfields, that the German commercial airlines were being organized in such a way that they could easily be converted into a powerful military air force, and that schemes were being hatched for quietly setting up munitions factories—all in violation of the Treaty of Versailles. The article also blasted the Ministry of Transportation for preparing a new war strategy involving quick strikes and rapid transportation.

Unfortunately, nothing came of this disclosure except seven more months in prison for Ossietzky. Not wanting diplomatic relations in Europe to be spoiled by controversy, the countries that were in a position to enforce the Versailles treaty did not act on the reports of German rearmament.

After being arrested again in 1931 for publishing an article that criticized the function of soldiers, Ossietzky spoke out

Adolf Hitler projected the image of a strong man who would restore Germany to its former glory, but Ossietzky recognized him for the tyrant he was.

bitterly against the weakness of the Weimar republic. He feared that the government's failure to take command of Germany left the way open for more militaristic people to take over.

While Ossietzky was warning of the dangers of a weak government, another man was promising to rebuild the German military and restore prosperity to Germany. The German people were intrigued by this rising newcomer, whose name was Adolf Hitler, but Ossietzky, who wrote that Hitler was a coward, was quick to sense that there was something evil about the man. Ossietzky's fears were realized when the militarists he had warned about played upon the weakness of the government to help Hitler seize control of Germany. As Hitler's Nazis— the National Socialist German Workers' Party—gained more power, Ossietzky began to concentrate his attack on the party and *der Führer* (the Leader), as Hitler had come to call himself.

By the end of 1932, Germany was held in the tight grip of the Nazis. Joseph Goebbels, the minister of **propaganda,** had absolute control over the press, and editors were expected to print what Goebbels wanted printed and to stay away from publishing what he banned. The government declared it to be a crime to publish anything against government interests.

There was no hope for survival for a firebrand such as Ossietzky in this kind of setting. He would not compromise his ever. On February 27, 1933, the Nazis used the excuse of an arson incident to crack down on all "enemies of the state." More than 4,000 writers, lawyers, and other critics of the government—including Ossietzky—were pulled out of their homes by Nazi storm troopers and thrown into prison without any trials.

A Light in the Darkness

Ossietzky was offered his release if he would sign a pledge to stop writing about political subjects, an offer he wouldn't even consider. More than 50,000 German citizens signed a petition asking that he be given his freedom, but they were ignored. For the next five years, Ossietzky was hidden away from public view in concentration camps.

The journalist's courage, however, had touched people throughout the world. As the truth about the Nazis and their methods began to leak out, 21 nations and 6 past Nobel Peace Prize winners filed petitions asking that "the prize be sent into a concentration camp" and be given to Ossietzky. This put the Norwegians, the custodians of the prize, in a precarious position. Many feared that in awarding the prize to one of Hitler's greatest enemies, the Norwegians would enrage the Nazis to the point that they might attack Norway. In the end, a change had to be made declaring that members of the Nobel awards committee could not

This Nazi propaganda poster tried to convince people that Germany's victory was Europe's freedom.

beliefs about freedom of thought and expression. Friends urged him to leave the country before it was too late, but Ossietzky refused. "It is a hollow voice that speaks from across the border," he declared. He would stay in his native country and demand that it listen to him.

After serving a jail term for exposing government secrets, Ossietzky published articles that were more provoking than

23

also be government members. In that way, the awarding of the 1935 Nobel Peace Prize to Carl von Ossietzky could not be taken as a statement of Norwegian foreign policy.

Hitler's government reacted bitterly, calling Ossietzky a traitor and the award a shameless insult. *Der Führer* struck back at the Nobel action by declaring that no German citizen could accept a Nobel Prize, not even in the areas of science and literature. But Ossietzky

defied the Nazis to the very end. Even though the years of torture and isolation had left him physically and mentally broken, Ossietzky insisted on his right to the prize. German officials, however, refused to allow him to leave the country to accept the award in person. Ossietzky paid the ultimate price in the fight for peace and freedom of expression when he failed to survive the rigors of imprisonment beyond 1938. As an extra measure of injustice, Ossietzky's lawyer embezzled nearly all of his client's prize money.

Carl von Ossietzky did not live to see the horrible consequences of the military buildup and the Nazi philosophy that he had warned against. But he would not have been surprised that these policies were partially responsible for plunging the world into the most terrible war it had ever known, World War II, in which an estimated 55 million people lost their lives. Adolf Hitler turned out to be a greater menace than even Ossietzky could have imagined. Not only did he lead the Nazis in their attack on Europe, but his insane prejudices against Jews and other minority groups also led to the mass murder of more than 6 million innocent people.

Ossietzky could point to no tangible results from his sacrifices for peace. But the courage of this German writer, whose name is barely known in most of the world, has led observers to call him the "outstanding hero of peace in modern times." Carl von Ossietzky stood as a shining example of civilization when peace was disappearing from much of the world, and he kept the light of peace burning during a time of impenetrable darkness.

Nazi madness allowed Hitler to be a friend to one group of children (left) while thousands of other children were herded into concentration camps to await their deaths (right).

The giant mushroom cloud of a nuclear explosion releases dangerous radioactive fallout into the atmosphere.

3

Linus Pauling versus the Bomb

A row of scientists lay flat on the ground at the bleak, remote desert site of Alamogordo Air Force Base in New Mexico. Nervously they awaited the countdown to the event that would make July 16, 1945, one of the most ominous turning points in history. Even the most knowledgeable scientist could not have fully imagined the force that was about to be unleashed on that Monday morning. Searing sheets of light that were visible for over 180 miles ripped through the sky, drowning out the sunlight. Minutes later, hurricane-force winds rushed with an unearthly roar over the trembling observers. The scientists had witnessed the first atomic bomb explosion.

27

Less than a month later, on August 6, 1945, the United States bomber *Enola Gay* cruised over the island empire of Japan. The skies over the city of Hiroshima were perfectly clear, the conditions ideal for dropping the deadly cargo. The doors of the bomb bay opened, a single, ponderously heavy cylindrical object rolled out, and the airplane sped away. This atomic bomb exploded with even more force than the test bomb at Alamogordo. All buildings within a half-mile radius of the explosion were reduced to ashes, and a huge, mushroom-shaped cloud billowed over the city, a monument marking the graves of more than 100,000 victims.

These two explosions ushered the world into the terrifying age of nuclear power. The threat posed by weapons like the atomic bomb gave new meanings to the concepts of war and peace. Never before had humans had the power to almost instantaneously destroy the entire human race. This truly was the force that Alfred Nobel was referring to when he spoke of weapons so powerful that nations would dare not risk even the thought of war. But the improvement of weapons had never before in history lessened the likelihood of destruction, and nuclear weapons were no exception.

After World War II, as the superpowers busily fashioned a new generation of nuclear weapons 1,000 times more powerful and frightening than the atomic bomb dropped on Hiroshima, it seemed that the world

A single atomic bomb dropped from the **Enola Gay** *(above) destroyed the city of Hiroshima on August 6, 1945 (left).*

was marching blindly toward oblivion.

"What Have We Done?"

The first to grasp the consequences of the new age of weapons were the people who had created it: scientists. It was the genius Albert Einstein who pointed out that scientists found themselves in the very spot where Nobel had stood when he invented dynamite. According to Einstein, because of scientists' contributions to nuclear technology, it was their duty to warn the world of the danger it faced.

One of those who responded to the call was an American scientist named Linus Pauling. Born in Oregon in 1901, Pauling had risen to the top of the scientific profession and had himself been involved in developing weapons for the United States. During World War II, his work as a member of the explosives division of the National Defense Resources Committee had earned him a Presidential Medal of Merit. In 1946, Pauling joined seven other scientists in forming the Emergency Committee of Atomic Scientists, which worked with other organizations, such as the 2,000-member Federation of American Scientists, to inform the public about the devastation that the powerful new weapons could cause.

While American scientists were warning of the dangers of nuclear weapons, the Soviets were developing an atomic bomb of their own. In the late 1940s and in the 1950s, as relations between the United States and the Soviet Union grew more and more strained, fearful Americans did not want to risk having less military power than the Soviets. More than two-thirds of the people in the United States opposed any kind of **disarmament** talks. Those who supported the reduction of weapons were thought to be trying to help the Soviet Union and ran the risk of being labeled Communists.

Pauling and a small minority of concerned people ignored public sentiment and carried on with their mission, explaining the urgent need for new approaches to settling international conflict. It was Pauling who, in 1947, warned of the development of the hydrogen bomb, an even more devastating weapon than the bomb that had destroyed Hiroshima. But the United States government, which was not yet ready to listen to warnings about nuclear weapons, saw Pauling as a trouble-maker. The scientist was denied a passport in 1952, and even his triumph of winning the 1954 Nobel Prize for chemistry did not improve his reputation in the eyes of the government.

Pauling's cause gained support as the truth in what he was saying gradually became obvious. By 1952, the United States had successfully tested a hydrogen bomb, and the Soviet Union followed close behind. This further escalation of the arms race stirred up more scientists to join Pauling's fight for peace. In July of 1955, Pauling was only one of many who signed the Einstein-Russell Appeal, which asked that nations set aside emotions and realize that their survival depended on cooperation. That same month, Pauling joined 52 Nobel laureates in calling on all nations to renounce the use of force in their dealings with each other.

The Invisible Menace

As the number of test bombs set off increased, Pauling began to focus his energies on one little-understood side effect of the nuclear arms race—**nuclear fallout.** Fallout is the poisonous radiation released during a nuclear explosion. Few people knew anything at all about fallout during the 1950s, and fewer still were concerned about it. The United States Civil Defense Administration published a pamphlet that described fallout as "only particles of matter in the air." The administration reassured the public that fallout was not dangerous because "the whole world is radioactive." *Life* magazine published the hopeful opinion that "radiation may even be helpful." In 1957, the *New York Daily News* went so far as to advise readers to "laugh off" the warnings about fallout, claiming that scientists had found it to be harmless.

This last article was more than Linus

In an appearance before a Senate subcommittee, Pauling argues in favor of a ban on nuclear testing.

advice of the thousands of scientists who had signed the document, a Senate subcommittee wanted to know how Pauling had collected the names, who had helped him, and what connections he had with the Communist movement.

Meanwhile, the number of nuclear tests multiplied, filling the air with invisible clouds of poison that drifted into countries all over the world. By 1952, the United States had exploded a total of 16 nuclear weapons, the Soviet Union 2. By 1958, the United States had increased its test blasts to 52, the Soviets' total had ballooned to 25—including the most powerful bombs yet tested—and the British had chipped in with 5 tests of their own.

As the number of tests increased, so did Pauling's efforts to stop them. Among his estimates of the effects of nuclear fallout were figures showing that an atomic bomb blast of one megaton (an explosion equal to that of one million tons of TNT) could cause 1,000 cases of cancer. An expert in the field of genetic mutation, Pauling also pointed out the terrible effects that small levels of radiation could have on children and developing embryos. There were some scientists, especially in the United States, who disputed Pauling's claims, but many more came to his defense, including a group of Soviet scientists. Pauling's supporters declared the current spree of nuclear tests to be a crime against the future and said that if the tests went on unabated, they

Pauling could take. In just two months, he was able to gather the signatures of 3,000 United States scientists and 8,000 scientists from other countries on a document that stated that fallout was dangerous and urged that nuclear tests be stopped. Pauling's efforts met with the kind of reaction that so often confronts peace advocates. Instead of heeding the

31

would be paid for, by the scientists' calculations, with the lives of seven million people in each generation.

Pauling kept the subject of nuclear fallout in the news by filing suit in June 1958 against the United States Secretary of Defense, the Atomic Energy Commission, and the Soviet Minister of Defense. He called for a court injunction banning all nuclear tests in the atmosphere. Once brought out of the shadows, the ominous nature of this hidden killer, which could seep from the streams and plants of the earth into the bodies of animals and eventually collect, undetected, in humans, succeeded in jolting the public out of its indifference. That year, the percentage of Americans favoring some kind of disarmament was more than double what it had been 12 years earlier. This time the government authorities took heed of the complaints, and in 1958, all three countries that had been testing nuclear weapons in the atmosphere—the United States, the Soviet Union, and Great Britain—agreed to put a stop to it.

Starting Over Again

That triumph, however, lasted only as long as it took France to enter the nuclear age by exploding a test bomb in 1960, starting a new wave of nuclear explosions. The Soviet Union jumped in first, setting out on a series of 31 tests in 1961, which included a 50-megaton explosion that discharged a 500-mile-wide cloud of fallout into the air. The United States quickly answered with a rapid series of smaller blasts of its own. By 1962, the test bombs were blowing off at a rate of one every three days. The United States contributed 86 such tests for a total of 37 megatons, while the Soviet Union set off 40 far more powerful ones totaling about 180 megatons.

Refusing to be discouraged, Pauling resumed his fight in every way he could. He called public attention to measurements showing that the 1962 round of tests had more than doubled the amount of nuclear debris in the atmosphere. He noted the increase in radiation levels in plants and cautioned that radioactive substances were being concentrated to harmful levels in cow's milk. To those who said that the figures he was quoting were still under the government's allowable standards, Pauling answered that whenever the standards had been exceeded, the government had responded by simply raising the allowable standards.

Pauling wrote letters to leaders of both the Soviet Union and the United States, resumed his lawsuits against both countries, and picketed the United Nations building and the White House. Although he had been evenhanded in condemning the Soviet Union's test policy as well as that of the United States, many of his fellow Americans branded him a traitor, a crackpot, and a Communist. The scientist shrugged off such criticism without

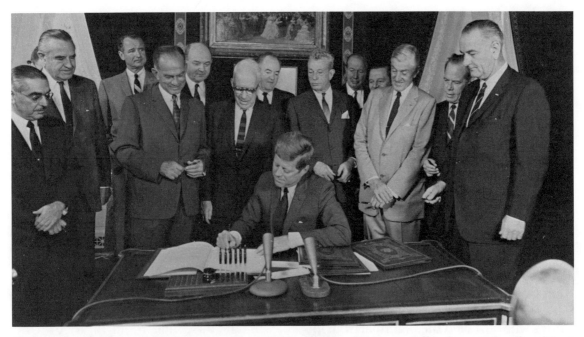

The persistent Pauling (front, second from left) sees his efforts pay off as he watches President John F. Kennedy sign the 1963 Limited Test Ban Treaty.

much comment and continued to voice his protests in more than 100 articles and in lectures delivered in 26 countries.

A rare, supremely satisfying moment in the history of peacemaking arrived on July 25, 1963. The two superpowers—the United States and the Soviet Union—along with Great Britain and many other nations that did not yet have nuclear capability, signed the Limited Test Ban Treaty. In the treaty, the countries agreed not to explode nuclear test devices on the ground, in space, or under water, although they could still set off the bombs underground. One year before the treaty was

signed, Linus Pauling was awarded the Nobel Peace Prize for his work to stop the testing of nuclear weapons.

As the stockpile of nuclear weapons continues to grow to the point that the earth could be destroyed many times over, the protests of Pauling and other concerned people cannot be said to have eliminated the possibility of annihilation. But the threat that future generations will be harmed by the proliferation of nuclear tests has been reduced, not by the actions of government negotiators, but because of worldwide protests by people like Linus Pauling.

4

Martin Luther King, Jr., versus the Invisible Chains

They came in chains, kidnapped from their homes and crammed into filth and darkness at the bottom of slave ships. Those who survived the nightmarish trip across the Atlantic found themselves transplanted from their native Africa to the "land of freedom"—the American colonies, which later became the United States of America. But there was no freedom awaiting these dark-skinned people, only slavery.

In 1865, the 13th Amendment was added to the Constitution, officially ending 200 years of slavery in the United States. But the 4.4 million blacks living in the nation at that time were not really free; they had only exchanged their visible chains for the invisible chains of prejudice and discrimination.

A white attitude of superiority resulted in laws and policies of **segregation** designed to keep blacks subordinate to whites. During the early 1900s, South Carolina prohibited textile factories from allowing black and white employees to work in the same room or to use the same doorways, stairs, bathrooms, or even pails. Oklahoma had separate phone booths for blacks and whites, and until 1940, blacks and whites in Atlanta, Georgia, could not visit the zoo at the same time. In the years during and after World War I, when blacks flocked to northern cities in search of better conditions, whites in the North joined those in the South in keeping the nation's 20 million black citizens out of white neighborhoods and churches, schools and workplaces, cemeteries and voting booths.

King arrives in Washington, D.C., in August 1963 to demonstrate that the time for racial equality is now.

A Rebellion is Sparked

In December of 1955, a weary Rosa Parks rode the city bus home from work in Montgomery, Alabama. Parks, who was black, was seated in the first row of the section at the back of the bus where blacks were required by law to sit. When the white section had filled up, she was ordered to give up her seat to a white rider. Parks refused and was arrested and fined $10. This incident sparked a rebellion against the humiliating treatment that blacks had endured for centuries. Among those stirred to action was the pastor of the Dexter Avenue Baptist Church, a black man named Martin Luther King, Jr.

King was born in Atlanta, Georgia, in 1929. A brilliant student, King graduated from high school at age 15 and went on to earn a doctorate in theology. After the Rosa Parks incident, the black community of Montgomery decided to organize a **boycott** of the city's buses and asked the 26-year-old pastor, who had been on the job only a year, to be their leader. When King agreed, it was the beginning

NO SPITTING

COLORED
PASSENGERS

When Rosa Parks (left) refused to give up her seat on a Montgomery bus to a white rider, she inspired blacks to demand equal rights.

of a movement that would change the course of a nation.

In one of his first speeches during the Montgomery crisis, King impressed listeners with his call for their protests to remain true to "the highest principles of law and order." Combining his firm belief in the ideals of Christianity with the techniques of India's leader of nonviolent protest, Mohandas Gandhi, King urged his listeners to engage in a moral battle against injustice without resorting to violence. He believed that the force of a mass of people united peacefully in a just cause would eventually win out over violence and hatred.

The Montgomery bus boycott provided plenty of opportunities to test King's theory. For 382 days, blacks refused to ride the city buses. Those who had cars filled them up with riders; others walked miles to and from work every day to support the protest. Not only did the buses lose fares, but businesses in Montgomery also began to lose money because their black customers had stopped riding the buses downtown to shop.

The effectiveness of the boycott caused a storm of resentment in the white community. Blacks were insulted, cursed, threatened, and beaten. King himself was harassed at every turn by police and was even put in jail for driving five miles over the speed limit. Obscene and menacing phone calls poured in, and none of them could be taken lightly after a bomb blast ripped apart King's home. The King family was fortunate to escape without serious injury.

Despite such abuse, King insisted that the black community would not be provoked into taking up weapons against their attackers. It was King's philosophy that the freedom fighters must take suffering on themselves rather than inflict it on others. In an incredible display of

37

restraint, the boycott was kept completely nonviolent on the part of the blacks until the Supreme Court of the United States ruled in 1956 that the Montgomery bus ordinance was unconstitutional and ordered the city buses to desegregate.

A New Vision of Hope

Under King's leadership, the bus boycott had accomplished two things: it had proven that the techniques of nonviolent protest could work in a Western democracy, and it had created a revolution in expectations among blacks in the United States. After the courageous stand in Montgomery, many blacks felt that they no longer had to tolerate the humiliation that had been heaped on their race for hundreds of years. Blacks who had held no hope for equality before they had heard King speak could not help but be stirred up by the vision of liberty and justice that he was preaching.

When King took on the awesome role of spokesperson for the **civil rights** movement, he realized that there was a long way to go and hard work ahead. With the growing influence of mass media, it was easier than ever to focus national attention on a cause; yet, when bombarded with a subject, the public was quick to tire of it. It was King's job to strike a careful balance between public awareness and overexposure. As a skilled orator and nonthreatening black leader,

King was able to let the white community know what blacks were going through. He appealed to their consciences to convince them of the justice in what blacks were asking.

In 1957, following through on the momentum of the Montgomery success, King helped organize and became president of the Southern Christian Leadership Conference (SCLC), a civil rights group composed mostly of black ministers. With his growing reputation as the most captivating public speaker of the time, King was in demand throughout the country. From 1957 to 1968, he traveled about six million miles and delivered more than 2,500 speeches. During this time, King also helped out in local civil rights campaigns, including protests in Georgia, Virginia, and North Carolina, and in Harlem, New York, where he suffered a serious knife wound at the hands of a deranged woman, a wound that forced him out of action for months.

Peace through Crisis

After a campaign in Albany, Georgia, failed to stimulate any real changes, King decided to use his enemies to advance his nonviolent pursuit of civil rights. He switched tactics from simply trying to arouse the conscience of the people to a strategy of purposely creating a crisis and letting the advocates of hatred and bigotry expose themselves. This new

Despite King's philosophy of never inflicting suffering on others, he was forced to spend many nights behind bars.

approach was used in 1963 when King and his staff plotted a bold move to challenge the racist policies of Birmingham, Alabama, sometimes called the "most segregated city in America."

King's conviction that the protesters should take suffering on themselves rather than inflict it on others was severely tested in Birmingham. Protest marches were met with shocking brutality as police attacked demonstrators with guard dogs and powerful blasts of water from fire hoses. Many people were hurt during the campaign, which lasted more than a month, and when a bomb was thrown into a Sunday school classroom, four young black girls were killed. In spite of King's pleas for restraint, some of Birmingham's blacks grew frustrated with the policy of nonviolence and struck back by rioting.

As the leader of the Birmingham protest, King himself was constantly threatened, occasionally attacked, and on more than 20 occasions, carted off to jail. Verbal attacks came from all sides, from blacks who criticized him for indecisiveness and compromise and for being too peaceful, as well as from whites who saw him not as a peaceful person but as a lawbreaker and a troublemaker. FBI director J. Edgar Hoover publicly branded King "the most notorious liar in the country."

Night after night, horrified television viewers witnessed the brutal treatment of the nonviolent marchers and could not help but sympathize with the blacks. National and international pressure stirred up by the inhumanity in Birmingham nudged Congress into considering passage of a federal civil rights bill proposed by President Kennedy. King helped to organize the March on Washington to urge the passage of the bill and call attention to black unemployment.

39

"I have a dream that my four little children will one day live in a nation where they will not be judged by the color of their skin but by the content of their character.
    I have a dream . . ."

Martin Luther King, Jr.
Washington, D.C.
August 28, 1963

40

The March on Washington took place on August 28, 1963, when more than 200,000 people—both black and white—marched from the Washington Monument to the Lincoln Memorial. King gave the gathering its most magical moment with his "I Have a Dream" speech in which he spoke of equality for all people. Not long after the demonstration, Congress passed the Civil Rights Act of 1964, which prohibited discrimination not only because of race, but also because of sex, religion, or national origin.

Just months after the Civil Rights Act was passed, Martin Luther King, Jr., was awarded the 1964 Nobel Peace Prize for demonstrating that nonviolent disobedience could be used to combat unjust laws. But in spite of the new law and the honors, King knew there was more work to be done.

King geared up for yet another crisis in early 1965. This time the issue was voting rights and the target was Selma, Alabama. In many counties in the South, authorities made it difficult for blacks to vote. Their methods included requiring that people pay a **poll tax** before being allowed to vote, which made voting much too expensive for many blacks. In the county where Selma was located, only 156 out of the 15,000 eligible black voters were registered to vote in 1961, and very little progress had been made since then.

As people gathered for a protest march from Selma to the Alabama state capital in Montgomery, they knew that racial prejudice ran so deeply in Selma that ugly, violent incidents were likely to happen. Just as they had expected, columns of marchers, including King, were attacked by state and local police as they walked toward Montgomery. Again, by taking suffering upon themselves, King's followers aroused the national conscience enough to pave the way for the Voting Rights Act, which was signed into law in August of 1965.

A Crusade Cut Short

In 1966, King and his family moved to Chicago to fight discrimination in the cities of the North as well as the South. While continuing to support the civil rights movement, King also began to speak out against the Vietnam War. On April 4, 1968, King was in Memphis, Tennessee, to lend support to striking black garbage workers when his nonviolent crusade was stopped abruptly by an act of violence—he was killed by an assassin's bullet.

Although his work was cut short, the campaigns Martin Luther King, Jr., had helped lead carved out visible improvements for blacks in the United States. In 1940, only 1 in 10 blacks completed high school. By 1989, the percentage of blacks graduating from high school was 36.5, and almost 12 percent of blacks over 25 had completed college. At the time

Hundreds of thousands of people, both black and white, gathered in Atlanta, Georgia, on April 9, 1968, to mourn the death of Martin Luther King, Jr.

that the Civil Rights Act of 1964 was being passed by Congress, there were only 103 black public officials elected to a national or a state office. By 1975, that figure had soared to over 3,500 and more than a million blacks who had been excluded from elections had begun to take advantage of their right to vote. By 1989, there were 7,191 blacks in public office.

The invisible chains of prejudice and discrimination are still with us and may never be gone for good. But in the march for peace, progress is measured not in miles but in footsteps, and Martin Luther King, Jr., brought the world a step closer to his dream of racial equality and harmony.

43

5

Andrei Sakharov
versus Mind Control

Through strange twists of fate, the Nobel Peace Prize has occasionally ended up in the hands of the most unlikely champions of peace. Past prizewinners include Theodore Roosevelt, a president who scoffed at pacifists and took pride in a powerful army; George Marshall, a general in the United States Army; Anwar Sadat and Menachem Begin, both former members of militant organizations; and Le Duc Tho and Henry Kissinger, the representatives of the two countries that ravaged Vietnam during the Vietnam War.

Perhaps the greatest irony connected with the Nobel Peace Prize is that this award created by the inventor of dynamite, Alfred Nobel, would one day be given to "the father of the Soviet H-bomb," Andrei Sakharov. Sakharov has had to live with the knowledge that he is largely responsible for developing the Soviet hydrogen bomb, a weapon so hideous that it endangers the existence of the world. But this man, who has probably explored more corners of the human conscience than anyone else of his time, has repaid the world by dedicating himself to the tortuous quest for peace and human rights, often in open defiance of the Soviet government.

The Soviet Union has been a frightening place for people who disagree with official government policy. At its worst, the government has employed tactics as

Nobel Prize winner Andrei Sakharov and his wife, Yelena Bonner

ruthless as those of Nazi Germany—as in the bloody purges periodically ordered by Joseph Stalin in the 1930s and 1940s during which he killed people indiscriminately. Even in more lenient times, the Soviet government has kept a tight grip on the thoughts and actions of its people.

In most **totalitarian** regimes, a dissenter is considered to be a political criminal, but the Soviets carry it one step further. In the Soviet Union, dissent, which is called being "different minded," is not just a crime, but a sickness. To engage in repeated criticism of the government is thought of as a form of insanity, and this enables the government to justify what many westerners consider to be mind control. The policy is that dissenters, or the "insane," do not have the ability to function in society, so the state can make all their decisions for them and, in some cases, can confine them to psychiatric hospitals.

Father of the Soviet H-bomb

Andrei Sakharov grew up knowing the insecurity of living in a country where grave consequences await those who are even suspected of disagreeing with the government. Born in Moscow in 1921, four years after the Communist Revolution, Sakharov lost seven close relatives to the Soviet quest for internal security. Each was taken from his home, sent away to a prison camp, and never heard from again.

Sakharov's father was a well-known author and physics instructor, and he found his son to be a wonderful student. The boy mastered his lessons quickly and soon surpassed all of his teachers, including his father. As a college student during World War II, Sakharov showed a brilliance in solving physics and math problems that earned him a rare exemption from military service.

A few years after the war ended, Sakharov was put to work on a secret project for the government. From 1948 to 1958, the widely published physicist labored in seclusion with a team of researchers to perfect a devastating thermonuclear weapon, the hydrogen bomb. Although the history of that effort remains shrouded in silence, it is widely agreed that Sakharov made the major contribution. That opinion is supported by the fact that in 1953, the year in which the Soviet Union became the first country besides the United States to set off a hydrogen test bomb, Sakharov was rewarded with membership in the Soviet Academy of Sciences. At 32 years of age, he was the youngest person ever so honored.

To many Soviet citizens, boxed in by government bureaucracy and economic shortages, Andrei Sakharov seemed to have a perfect life. He could live where he wanted, enjoy comforts of life not available to most Russians, and work with the best minds and in the best facilities the country had to offer. He would suffer no guilt for being an accomplice to the development of the menacing hydrogen bomb as long as he believed that by matching the United States in nuclear capability, he had helped to deter the Western superpower from ever using the weapon against the Soviet Union.

Sakharov's comfortable environment soon turned into a stifling one, however, when he began to question the actions of the Soviet government. In 1958, he unsuccessfully urged Premier Nikita Khrushchev to abandon an educational program that would require top science students to get job experience working on farms and in factories. While unremarkable in itself, this small protest foreshadowed Sakharov's growing opposition to Soviet policies.

In 1961, mindful of the damage that a single test bomb could do to the environment, Sakharov urged the government to hold off on a series of aboveground test blasts scheduled for the following year. Of special concern was a 50-megaton blockbuster that would make the bomb that had destroyed Hiroshima during World War II look like a hand grenade. In a confidential letter, Sakharov warned

Neither Joseph Stalin (left) nor Nikita Khrushchev (right) left room for dissent in the Soviet societies they led.

47

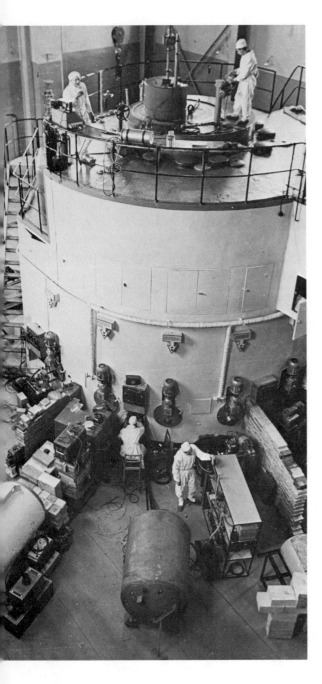

Khrushchev of the dangers of nuclear testing and asked that it be stopped. Officials assured Sakharov that the 50-megaton explosion would be called off, but privately Khrushchev observed that the brilliant physicist should keep his mind on physics and leave the government to those who knew how to run it. The frightful test went ahead as scheduled, leaving Sakharov with a feeling of betrayal and powerlessness.

Heartsick for Freedom

Quiet, almost timid by nature, Sakharov did not suddenly strike out on an anti-Soviet campaign. But as the years went by, he began to long for more freedom to express his thoughts than the Soviet system was willing to allow even a privileged scientist. Influenced by his contacts with humanitarians from the West, including Albert Schweitzer and Linus Pauling, Sakharov began to speak out against Soviet policies that he considered to be destructive.

In his protests, Andrei Sakharov pounded away on the theme of responsibility both for radioactive contamination from nuclear tests and for industrial pollution

Sakharov helped to bring the Soviet Union into the atomic age. This is an experimental atomic reactor at the Leningrad Physico-Technical Institute.

choking the waters and the air. He appealed for worldwide cooperation to control the nuclear weapons race to which he had once contributed. When the Soviet government, which had been relaxing its restrictions on political freedoms for its citizens, suddenly reversed itself in 1966 and arrested a group of freethinking writers, Sakharov boldly circulated petitions denouncing the crackdown.

Bolstered by his reputation as one of his country's greatest citizens, Sakharov was allowed to stray a bit further from official government positions than most. But it wasn't long before even a national hero like Sakharov had crossed the line into the forbidden zone. The first sign of trouble came with the publication of Sakharov's most famous writing, a **manifesto** entitled *Progress, Coexistence, and Intellectual Freedom,* in which he argued that world peace depended on the Soviet and United States political systems growing more and more alike. Sparing neither side in his critique, Sakharov's goal was to promote more humane governments that would totally reject the use of force or violence. Although well received around the world, Sakharov's manifesto prompted his own government to remove him from his research post in 1968.

By this time, however, Sakharov's passion for freedom could not be squelched. Gradually, his concern shifted from philosophical arguments to the very real plight of fellow citizens who were victims of the

Andrei Sakharov

government's intolerance of **dissidents**, people who opposed the government. At a time when few people outside of the Soviet Union were aware of a dissident movement in that country, Sakharov became one of the movement's leaders.

Answering letters from persecuted individuals and religious groups, writing appeals on their behalf to the authorities, keeping vigil at their trials, Sakharov lent

Yelena Bonner met Sakharov at a vigil outside a dissident's trial in 1970 and married him in 1971.

hope and inspiration to thousands of frightened men and women. He publicly scoffed at the "fair trials" that were held in secret and at the practice of putting dissidents in psychiatric hospitals. Along with two other people, Sakharov founded the Committee for Human Rights in the Soviet Union in 1970. This group called for freedom of the press, an end to secret trials, **amnesty** for all political prisoners, prison reform, and the abolition of the death penalty.

Freedom Crushed

Slowly, the government began to tighten the vise around the "different-minded" people. One by one, they picked up Sakharov's friends for interrogation, trial, and sentencing. By 1973, the Soviet KGB (secret police) had dismantled the Committee for Human Rights and crushed the movement. Sakharov was brought before a top government prosecutor and sternly warned against any more criticism of the government or any contact with foreign journalists.

But the embittered physicist knew that the only hope for the survival of the movement rested with those foreign journalists. The Soviet system allowed no avenues for pursuing the reforms he wanted. All he could do was to keep the issues in the news so that other countries would put pressure on his government to act humanely. Immediately after receiving his warning from the prosecutor, Sakharov called a news conference. Far from backing away from his positions, he said the United States should demand more freedom for Soviet citizens as a price for continuing cooperative ventures with the Soviet Union.

Sakharov was eventually shorn of all his special privileges and scientific challenges and faced constant harassment, but he continued to work for human rights. His cause was championed by Russian emigrants to the West, including the writer Alexander Solzhenitsyn, and in 1975, Sakharov became the first Russian citizen to win the Nobel Peace Prize. This further infuriated the Soviet heads of state, and Sakharov was not permitted to attend the Nobel ceremonies.

Sakharov finally fell from his precarious position as a public dissenter in January of 1980. Three weeks after he had condemned the Soviet invasion of Afghanistan, his car was stopped in the middle of a busy street and he was seized by KGB agents. Because of repeated "anti-Soviet" activities, Sakharov was banished from his home in Moscow and flown 250 miles to the city of Gorki. There he was kept under close watch, far from foreign reporters and deprived of telephone communication. He was even forced to carry his manuscripts with him wherever he went to keep them from being destroyed by the police. Slowly, Sakharov began to slip into the shadows of the Soviet system.

For years, sketchy reports and rumors were all that escaped from Gorki concerning Andrei Sakharov. Then late in 1986, the Soviet Union suddenly announced that Sakharov would be allowed to return to his home in Moscow with his wife, Yelena Bonner, and resume his work in physics. Upon his release, it was immediately apparent that although the seven years of exile had taken their toll on Sakharov's health, they had done nothing to break his spirit. Andrei Sakharov made no secret of the fact that, whatever the consequences, he would continue to voice his beliefs and support the human rights movement. Up until his death on December 14, 1989, Andrei Sakharov pursued the goal of world peace and brought international attention to the need for reform in his country.

6

Betty Williams & Mairead Corrigan versus Religious Terrorism

On August 10, 1976, Anne Maguire decided that her family needed a break from the confinement of their home in Belfast, Northern Ireland, so she took three of her four children, ages 8, 2½, and 6 weeks, for a walk. Maguire, who was Catholic, knew that the streets were not always safe in Belfast where hostile feelings between Roman Catholics, Protestants, and British soldiers occasionally burst into violence. But who would harm a mother with three young children?

As the Maguires walked through the streets, the quiet of the neighborhood was suddenly shattered by the all-too-

IRA supporters stone a British soldier while protesting Queen Elizabeth's visit to Northern Ireland in 1977.

familiar sound of gunshots echoing off the walls of the buildings. A carload of members of the Irish Republican Army (IRA)—an underground military organization—had surprised a group of British soldiers, fired their weapons, and roared off through the streets to avoid capture. Recovering quickly, the soldiers raced after the car, shooting as they gave chase. The driver was shot and slumped dead at the wheel while the speeding car rocketed out of control. An instant later, the unmanned vehicle slammed into the terrified Maguire family.

Anne Maguire suffered serious injuries but eventually recovered, at least physically. Nothing, however, could ever begin to heal the wound left by the loss of three of her children, who were killed in the collision.

Closed Neighborhoods

Northern Ireland is home to about 1.5 million people. Roughly 1 million of these belong to the Protestant faith while the remaining 500,000 are Roman Catholic. Throughout most of the world, Protestants and Catholics have learned that the barriers that separate them are not worth fighting over. In Northern Ireland, however, the problems have gone beyond simple differences in religion. Many people feel that being Protestant in Northern Ireland brings better jobs, more power in government, and more status in society than being Catholic. Even in the 1980s, help-wanted ads have specified whether the employer was interested in hiring a Protestant or a Catholic. The differences have developed into a huge, often-violent split that has caused each side to withdraw into its own closed neighborhoods.

The tragedy suffered by the Maguire family was the product of an accumulation of injustices that had been nursed along for decades in Northern Ireland and for centuries in Ireland. For hundreds of years, Protestants held most of the power in Ireland while Catholics made up the majority of the population. Ireland had been part of Great Britain for well over 100 years when the British government divided the island into two sections in 1920: the predominantly Catholic south and the mostly Protestant north. This compromise, which was designed to safeguard the interests of the Protestant minority in Ireland, created a new minority within the six counties of the north: Catholics, whose interests were largely ignored.

In 1949, the southern part of Ireland declared itself independent from Great Britain and became the Republic of Ireland. Fed up with their second-class status, many Catholics in Northern Ireland longed to be united with the new republic in one independent Ireland. Most Protestants, however, were proud to be British subjects and were not eager to be thrown into a Catholic-dominated society.

Inspired by the success of civil rights campaigns in the United States, Northern Ireland's Catholics became more vocal in their demands for equal rights in the 1960s. The Catholic and Protestant communities, however, insulated from each other by decades of prejudice, were unable to work out any solutions. Catholics, joined by Protestants who were sympathetic to their cause, planned a protest march in 1968, which the Protestant-dominated government prohibited. When the protesters defied the ban, the smoldering hatreds burst out in violence. Before long, incidents of rock throwing, vandalism, and gunfire were becoming more and more common.

British soldiers called in to restore peace were at first welcomed by Catholics as protection against Protestant extremists. But as Protestant attacks diminished, the soldiers who stayed were seen by

Catholics as the oppressors—foreign troops occupying their land in order to enforce unfair laws. Paramilitary groups such as the Irish Republican Army (Catholic) and the Ulster Defense Association (Protestant) were responsible for such terrorist actions as bombings and assassinations. The fighting continued to accelerate, and in 1971, 800 violent incidents claimed the lives of 31 soldiers and 71 civilians during only four months. Any Catholic or Protestant who ventured into the wrong neighborhood risked death or injury. By the time Anne Maguire took her fateful stroll, more than 1,600 people, mostly civilians, had been killed since the acceleration of violence in 1968.

Out of the Shock—A Plan

As the news of the Maguire accident spread across Northern Ireland, a shocked television audience focused on the dead children's grief-stricken aunt, Mairead Corrigan. Her tearful condemnation of violence on both sides hit an emotional nerve in a people used to stories of bloodshed and violence. At the same time, Betty Williams, a witness to the accident, was driven to a relentless effort to stop the destruction. A Catholic and former IRA supporter, Williams worked until past 2:00 A.M. on the morning after the accident collecting 6,000 signatures in support of immediate peace in Northern Ireland. Corrigan learned of Williams's efforts and

A group of children play under a Protestant "No Surrender" sign in Londonderry.

invited her to the children's funeral.

Although there had never before been an effective peace movement in Northern Ireland and neither Corrigan nor Williams

55

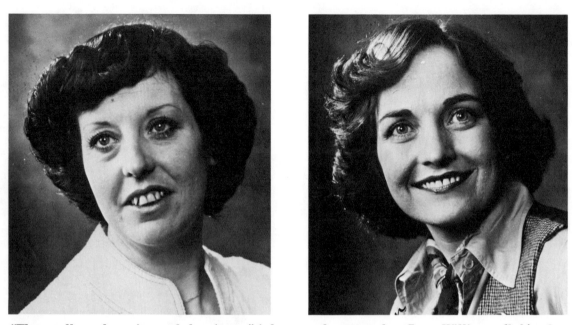

"They call us the saint and the sinner," jokes tough, outspoken Betty Williams (left) when speaking of gentle Mairead Corrigan (right) and herself.

had any training for organizing such a thing, they decided to work together to stop the fighting in their country.

In many ways the two women are opposites. Corrigan is the more typical pacifist. A kindhearted, religious person, she can see the good in nearly every situation. Williams, on the other hand, has described herself as being "the most aggressive person you'll ever meet in your life" and "not one bit nice." Her tough, stubborn personality has helped see her cause through some rough times.

Corrigan and Williams had to overcome an especially difficult problem in order to even begin to convince people to go along with a peace plan. The barriers separating Catholics and Protestants had become so thick that they were practically immovable. For people on each side, years of suffering terrible losses at the hands of extremists on the other side had fostered a war mentality, and the very thought of sitting down and talking with the hated enemy seemed like treason. The two women realized that to combat this environment their efforts must avoid any connection with organized religion or politics.

It seemed that their first demonstration—a march by 50 Catholic women protesting the activities of paramilitary organizations—would fail to include the all-important mix of Catholics and Protestants. But Williams and Corrigan, with help from journalist Ciaran McKeown, invited people from both sides to join them in their march through Belfast, the capital of Northern Ireland. Even though the march wound through Catholic areas, both Catholics and Protestants joined in until the ranks had swelled to 10,000, mostly women.

Accompanying themselves with non-sectarian hymns and prayers, the protesters bravely marched on, even when their way was barred by a growing crowd of militants. Many of the marchers were attacked with fists, rocks, and sticks, mostly at the hands of teenagers who had been raised to know only hatred of the other side. But the "Peace People," as they came to call themselves, refused to be bullied off the streets. They kept

Betty Williams (wearing dark glasses) and Ciaran McKeown (right of Williams) walk with the Peace People to a 1976 rally in London. Williams's husband and daughter are directly in front of her.

This wall, complete with barbed wire, divides the Catholic section of Belfast from the Protestant section.

marching and singing while both Catholics and Protestants protected their fellow marchers as best they could. Seeing their courage, some of the attackers were overcome with guilt and ended up joining the march.

Crossing the Barrier

The next step was to cross the barrier that divided Catholic Belfast from the Protestant neighborhoods. This meant marching through an area where few people dared venture, even in daylight. Over 35,000 Catholic and Protestant volunteers took up the challenge, however. In the next few months, Williams and Corrigan helped to organize a demonstration every weekend. More than 20,000 took part in a march through Londonderry, the most bitterly segregated of all Northern Ireland towns, and 30,000 people marched in Dublin, the capital of the

Republic of Ireland. Although many peace protesters came away from the demonstrations with bumps and bruises, they also learned a valuable lesson. For many it was their first real contact with a person of the other faith, and marches ended in tears and hugs as the protesters realized how much they had in common.

Williams and Corrigan were considered traitors by many people and put up with more than their share of abuse. But even when Williams and her children were beaten, they refused offers of protection. Betty Williams's gritty attitude showed in her answer to a bomb threat phoned in to her at 1:00 A.M. "Hurry up with it so I can get my sleep," she snapped.

By the end of March 1977, the Peace People had gathered more than 300,000 signatures on their Declaration of Peace, and Corrigan and Williams had even paid a visit to the United States to ask its citizens to stop sending money to paramilitary organizations. Having brought their cause to the attention of the public, they let the headline-making rallies stop and buckled down to the hard work of organizing a peace network. With 8,000 volunteers working on 110 peace committees, a grass-roots campaign was started to get people to break out of their tight neighborhoods and get to know the "enemy." The committees encouraged businesses to move in and provide economic opportunities in riot-torn neighborhoods. In one successful case, a woman opened a stationery plant and leather goods store in an area where no one else would build.

For their efforts in making it at least possible for groups in Northern Ireland to work for peace, Mairead Corrigan and Betty Williams were awarded the 1976 Nobel Peace Prize. The strife in their country is far from over, but the women haven't given up their fight. Total victories are hard to come by in the battle for peace. But like their more violent counterparts, the many bloody guerrilla campaigns throughout the world, Corrigan, Williams, and their "guerrillas for peace" hope to outlast the forces that oppose them.

60

7

Lech Walesa
versus the Party Bosses

The crucial turning points of history do not always spring out of situations as dramatic as the desperation of an infantry charge, the intensity of delicate negotiations, or the heat of a riot. Sometimes the destiny of an entire nation can suddenly be changed by an act as insignificant as taking a bit too long to finish a glass of beer.

In 1967, a restless 24-year-old Pole grew weary of trying to make a living as a garage mechanic in the small town of Lochocin. Hearing that there were better job opportunities elsewhere in Poland, Lech Walesa boarded a train bound for

Dressed as always like a common worker, Polish labor leader Lech Walesa holds a flower thrown to him by a supporter.

the city of Gdynia to seek his fortune. Before reaching Walesa's destination, the train stopped briefly in the city of Gdansk, part of a seaside metropolitan area that was home to about 850,000 people. Walesa figured there was just enough time to drink a glass of beer before moving on. His calculations were wrong, however, and the train rolled out of the station without him. Rather than wait for the next train, the young man stayed in Gdansk and found work at the sprawling Lenin Shipyard.

That fateful decision put Walesa in the center of the storm three years later. On December 12, 1970, Poles were preparing to celebrate the Christmas season when the government made an announcement that dampened their festive spirits. Effective immediately, food prices were doubled. Shocked at this sudden hardship, 10,000 angry workers in Gdansk took to the streets to protest. Walesa, who was one of the leaders of the workers, urged the group to remain calm, but in the end the protest deteriorated into a riot. On the last of three days of rioting, soldiers fired into a crowd of protesters, killing four people. After watching his fellow workers die in the streets, Lech Walesa would never be the same again.

Cloud of Misfortune

The episode proved that the cloud of misfortune that has hung over Poland since the country was officially recognized by the Vatican as a nation in 966 has not abated. Located in an area of

Much of Poland, including this section of Warsaw, was reduced to rubble by its stronger neighbors, Germany and the Soviet Union, during World War II.

productive farmland between Germany and Russia, Poland has continually attracted the armies of greedy neighbors eager to claim the country as their own. With no natural barriers such as mountains, large rivers, or deserts to protect them, the Poles have been caught in a vise between the powerful countries of Germany and the Soviet Union. No sooner would they get rid of one occupying army than another would invade.

The Poles regained their independence after World War I only for their land to be chopped up again in World War II. They were occupied first by Nazi Germany and then by the Soviet Union, which helped to establish a Communist government in Poland. Since then, Poland has remained under the domination of the Soviet Union. Its government has been run by Communist party officials who have forced the Poles to build monuments to the Soviet invaders, have tried to separate the intensely religious Poles from their cherished Roman Catholic church, and have greatly restricted other freedoms. Gross government mismanagement by the Communist party "bosses" has left the once-prosperous nation of almost 40 million people with grim economic problems.

Until Lech Walesa arrived on the scene, there was no way to safeguard the rights of individuals in Poland, particularly workers. Walesa was born in Popowo, Poland, in 1943. The son of a carpenter who died after being beaten and forced into hard labor by the Germans, he understood the despair of oppressed people. Walesa was never a brilliant student, but he was daring and willing to risk the wrath of authorities on occasion. Polish army supervisors, who reported that Walesa had enormous leadership potential, tried to enlist him in an officers' training program after his compulsary two years in the military. Walesa refused, however, preferring to remain in the working-class environment he had known all his life.

Walesa's natural leadership skills quickly surfaced at the Gdansk shipyards, where he worked as an electrician. He gained the trust of his fellow workers and was made a work inspector. This gave him freedom to go anywhere and talk to anyone at the plant, which helped him keep in touch with the wishes of a variety of workers.

Government officials, who became aware of Walesa's growing influence after the 1970 riots, had him watched and even tried to enlist him as an informer. Walesa refused and began to speak out about the government's lack of concern for the workers. After one such public protest in 1976, he was fired. Walesa, who was now married, was constantly turned away as a "troublemaker" in his efforts to find work to support his growing family. After months of part-time work as a mechanic, he would find a new job, then be fired for voicing a controversial opinion.

While employers did not appreciate Walesa, many of the common people did.

Striking Lenin Shipyard workers in Gdansk, Poland, sit under a poster showing the Soviet flag next to the Polish flag, a reminder that their powerful neighbor has its eye on them.

In spite of his problems keeping a job, Walesa remained active in the Free Trade Unions Movement, an underground organization devoted to—among other things—workers' rights, and was asked to address many meetings and rallies.

Solidarity

In July 1980, the Polish government announced a decision similar to the one that had set off riots 10 years earlier; they were going to raise food prices. This was viewed by the Poles not as a necessary policy but as merely the result of corruption and incompetence on the national level. Scattered strikes rose up across the country in protest. Meanwhile, at the Lenin Shipyard, a woman had been fired just five months before her retirement for missing work, even though she had the valid excuse of a bad illness. The time had come for the workers to stand up for their rights. It was Lech Walesa, out of work and now responsible for a wife and six children, who stood up in front of 6,000 cheering workers and declared a strike at the Lenin Shipyard.

Mindful of the disaster that had occurred 10 years before, Walesa insisted on orderliness and caution; for example, the use of alcoholic beverages was banned during the strike. Before long, the government gave in to the workers, granting them a healthy wage increase and restoring the woman and Walesa to their former jobs. But smaller groups of workers, who did not have the influence of the united mass of Gdansk laborers, were having a rougher time of it. Under Walesa's leadership, the shipyard workers went back on strike until their less-fortunate comrades were granted concessions.

Gradually, workers throughout the country were united in a single labor organization, which became known as Solidarity. As its leader, Walesa became the spokesperson for more than 10 million Poles and the inspiration for millions who longed for the freedoms for which Solidarity was fighting. Walesa's home became a beehive of activity as workers came to him for help in voicing their complaints.

In standing up to a government backed by the Soviet superpower, which did not allow dissenting points of view, Walesa faced a nearly impossible situation. But there was something about his forcefulness and his confidence that brought the Polish people streaming to his side. With

Lech Walesa

his bushy mustache and dumpy, baggy clothes, he was hardly a dashing sight. When scolded about his appearance, however, he retorted, "I'm a worker and I will dress like one."

Walesa was the fuel behind the workers' campaign on all fronts. It was he who attracted the media and focused world attention on Poland's problems. His speeches and public appearances bolstered his people's confidence and gave them courage to hold to their beliefs. In negotiations with government officials, Walesa put them on the defensive by talking about their mismanagement, and he refused to back down in the face of government pressure.

While Walesa was negotiating with the government, he also tried to keep his own side from losing control and repeating the violence of 1970. He warned the workers that if they pushed too hard, none of their demands would be met and that strikes had to be used wisely and sparingly or they would only cause more hardships. What Walesa had in mind was the reform, not the destruction, of the Polish government system, which hid its inefficiencies behind meaningless slogans. He envisioned a country with a new sense of "patriotism, peace, responsibility, reason, sense, and order."

By the end of the summer, Solidarity had won a smashing victory. All of their demands for free speech, free trade unions, and better wages and working conditions were met, and at the same time, 6 of the top 11 government leaders were dismissed. Hearing the news, Walesa literally jumped for joy and, crying freely, led a rally in the singing of the national anthem.

A Step Too Far

Once they had tasted some freedom, the appetites of some Solidarity members were whetted for more. For the next 16 months, Walesa had to walk a high wire between the radicals within his union and the government officials determined to crush the movement. There were times when he was forced to rein in his hot-headed friends. For instance, when a monument to Soviet soldiers was smeared with white paint, Walesa offered to clean up the mess himself. He argued against violence, appealed for national reconciliation, and sometimes compromised with the government rather than force an issue. Occasionally, he was scolded for making deals for Solidarity without the union's official approval.

Walesa was not opposed, however, to challenging the government when he felt it was necessary, as he showed in a successful drive to block the proposed six-day work week. He also approved of a highway blockade by buses and trucks to protest yet another giant food price increase, fought government bullying of the press, and forced an investigation into beatings of Solidarity members in Bydgoszcz.

In December of 1981, overconfident radicals within Solidarity caused Walesa to lose his precarious balance when they called for a national referendum, or vote, on whether or not the Communist party in Poland should be replaced. The reaction of General Wojciech Jaruzelski, the head of the Polish Communist party, was brutally swift. The next day, Solidarity's offices were ransacked, its telephone lines were cut, and its leaders, including Walesa,

Although the Solidarity movement was banned, the longing for freedom could not be suppressed. Walesa joins others in giving the movement's victory salute in 1985.

were arrested. Tanks rumbled through the streets as Jaruzelski declared Poland to be under **martial law**.

Walesa was held in detention for 11 months. During this time Polish citizens, including women and children, were attacked and arrested by the government and Solidarity was declared illegal. On November 15, 1982, Walesa was allowed to return home but was constantly shadowed by police.

In 1983 Lech Walesa was awarded the Nobel Peace Prize. Solidarity was clearly still alive and the government was forced to end martial law. The following years were difficult economically and politically in Poland. Finally, in 1989, the government asked Walesa for his help. After lengthy negotiations, Solidarity was declared legal and elections opened to those not approved by the Communist Party. Then on December 9, 1990, Lech Walesa became the first elected President of Poland. Lech Walesa continues to be a symbol of freedom, pride, and—most of all—hope for the people of Poland.

67

8

Desmond Tutu
versus Apartheid

An Anglican priest named Trevor Huddleston walked through streets crammed with small, slapped-together shacks. As the man approached the shanty where young Desmond Tutu lived, he caught sight of the boy's mother. Desmond was about to witness an act of such wonder it would change his life. Before his very eyes, Huddleston tipped his hat to Mrs. Tutu.

Such a sight was beyond anything Desmond had ever imagined, for Huddleston was white, Mrs. Tutu was black, and the incident occurred in the country of South Africa. It happened in a land where blacks had marveled at their first sight of television, not in amazement at the innovative technology, but in shock at seeing a white face smiling at them and speaking

Desmond Tutu leads a group of mourners in a funeral procession.

in a respectful tone. Huddleston filled Tutu with the hope that one day the racist policies of South Africa could be brought to an end, and with the ambition to work toward that goal.

Racism, discrimination, and segregation are considered ugly words throughout most of the world and are almost universally condemned, but in South Africa, they are the law. Although the population of South Africa is only about 16 percent white and over 70 percent black (the remainder of the population is of Asian or mixed descent), the white minority has control of the government. The South African government has adopted a policy called **apartheid**, which is designed to keep the country's different racial groups apart from each other and has served to deny blacks many of their human rights.

Supporters of the South African government point out that, as far as human rights are concerned, there are other governments throughout the world that are more brutal and tyrannical than South Africa. Perhaps this is true, but what sets South Africa apart for special criticism is that it is a wealthy, educated country that proudly claims to be part of the "free" world. Yet it is the only such country where government policies are based on race and where the treatment of people as subhuman is written into the law.

"Solving" the Black Problem

Life was hardly easy for nonwhites in South Africa in the first half of the 1900s; racial discrimination was rampant, and a wide gap separated the well-to-do whites from the poverty-stricken blacks. Conditions became far worse, however, in 1948 when the Nationalist Party came to power and began the policy of apartheid, which was made up of laws that would guarantee that the gap between blacks and whites remained.

The South African government could not keep the different races apart from each other unless they could easily identify to what race a person belonged. Therefore, **pass laws** were developed to sort people into neatly defined categories. Under the pass laws, everyone had to have documents that described his or her racial heritage, but only blacks were required to carry their documents, or passes, with them at all times or risk

arrest. Once a person was identified as black, he or she became a candidate for discrimination. If it could be proven that a person had any nonwhite ancestors, no matter how distant, that person was classified as "colored" and, like the blacks, was not allowed the rights of whites.

The laws of apartheid shackled the nonwhites in ever-tightening chains. People of different races were not allowed to live in the same city with each other, much less the same house, and had to use separate public facilities. Because there were few jobs available in black areas, many blacks had to take jobs in white cities far from their families. But they couldn't live near whites, so at five o'clock every afternoon, there would be a stream of black workers leaving the city and traveling many miles to the seedy barracks set up for them. Workers whose families lived hundreds of miles away in designated black areas often only saw them once a year at Christmas vacation time.

Apartheid laws increased the government's power by giving the officials a free hand to do whatever they wished to their opponents. Anyone who spoke out against the government could be arrested as a subversive. Those suspected of being antigovernment could be held in jail indefinitely, without trial and without charges filed against them.

In 1959, because nonwhites greatly outnumbered whites in South Africa, the government set up an elaborate scheme to relocate the blacks. Black South Africans were divided into nine ethnic groups and assigned to small, barren chunks of land. Each of these areas, called **homelands**, had its own black government, but they were ultimately controlled by the white South African government. The plan also took away the blacks' rights to have anything to do with the government of South Africa as a whole; they weren't even allowed to vote. Although the 24 million blacks made up over 70 percent of the population of South Africa, only 13 percent of the land was set aside for them. The great bulk of the more productive land went to fewer than 5 million whites.

In order to carry out this policy, blacks were uprooted from their homes and transported to "ancestral areas," which most had never seen before. White South Africa hoped that the homelands would declare their independence from the rest of the country and leave South Africa to the whites.

Pleas for Reason

Desmond Mpilo Tutu, the son of a Methodist schoolteacher, was born in 1931 in the western part of the South African province of Transvaal. After attending a Swedish mission school, he converted to the Anglican faith because of his admiration for Trevor Huddleston, the white priest who had treated Mrs. Tutu with

Desmond Tutu

such respect. Desmond was 17 years old when the fate of his people was sealed with the election of the Nationalist Party.

Tutu came very close to escaping the problems of apartheid in the only way that most South African blacks can escape: by death. As a teenager, he was hospitalized with a case of tuberculosis so severe that he was bedridden for almost two years. During that time, Huddleston—now a bishop and Tutu's friend and mentor—did not let a day go by without visiting him.

71

At a funeral for 27 people shot by the police, Tutu condemns violence by both the police and rioters.

As soon as Tutu had recovered from his illness, he finished school and then taught for three years. In 1957, when he objected to changes made by the government in the education of black students, Tutu resigned from his teaching position and began to study theology. He was ordained an Anglican priest in 1961 and worked as a church curate for two years before going to London to continue his studies. After earning a master's degree in theology, Tutu lectured at a seminary and at a university in South Africa from 1967 to 1972 before returning to England as associate director of the Theological Education Fund.

It was while Tutu was in England, thousands of miles away from the racist environment of his native country, that he was able to completely free himself from the idea that he was inferior to others because he was black. Meanwhile, in South Africa, violent protests against government policies were becoming more and more common. In 1975, Tutu, a man who was committed to nonviolence, returned to South Africa to join the struggle against apartheid.

Although anger at the racist policies of the South African government had caused many to rethink their commitment to nonviolence, Desmond Tutu held firm. Tutu, who became a bishop in 1976, waged his campaign from the pulpit. A spellbinding preacher known for a playful sense of humor, he painted a picture of freedom, argued for the worth of the individual, and showed apartheid to be totally inconsistent with Christianity.

Tutu's eloquent pleas for justice won respect and brought new and greater challenges his way. In 1978, he was named general secretary of the South African Council of Churches (SACC), which represents 13 million South Africans. As head of the organization, Tutu was entitled to comfortable accommodations, but he rejected them to stay with his parishioners in the miserable conditions of the black slum of Southwest Township (Soweto, for short) outside of Johannesburg.

Turning his energy to the peaceful fight against injustice, Tutu directed his agency in efforts to support the victims of apartheid. In a land where those arrested have sometimes been tortured and killed, SACC provided valuable help in arranging visits to jails and giving legal services to those in trouble with the government, as well as offering spiritual and financial support to the families of those arrested.

Despite his small stature—he is only about 5'3"—and gentle nature, Desmond Tutu is not a weak man. There have been times when he has had to face down supporters of his own cause, as he did when he cooperated with the white government to help end a black boycott of schools. More often, though, Tutu has dug in his heels against the unfair policies of the South African government. Never one to cover up his thoughts with diplomatic language, Tutu once told whites that, considering the history of the country, it was a miracle that blacks would be willing to speak to any whites. He has spoken out in favor of civil disobedience and has called on foreign countries to put pressure on the South African government in any way they can. Among the plans he has supported is **divestment**, the process by which foreign countries would stop investing in South African businesses or in companies that did business in South Africa. Although he advocates peaceful change, Tutu has warned that time is running out for South Africa, that the country will find itself in a bloodbath if reforms are not made quickly.

This kind of talk has infuriated many white South Africans, who have struck back at him. Tutu has been called a subversive, has had his passport revoked, and has even spent time in jail. In 1982, the government refused to allow him to accept an honorary doctorate from Columbia University in New York, a plan that backfired when university representatives

Tutu tries, unsuccessfully, to arrange a meeting with South Africa's prime minister, Pieter Botha. The more the government refuses to listen to nonviolent leaders such as Tutu...

flew to South Africa to present the award. The government of South Africa remained grimly silent when Tutu's words stirred enough international admiration to win the Nobel Peace Prize in 1984, but a progovernment newspaper scoffed that Tutu "stands for anything but peace."

The Dim Hope

Desmond Tutu is not the first person to fight against apartheid, nor is he the first to win a Nobel Peace Prize for doing

so. In 1960, a Zulu chief named Albert Luthuli was awarded the prize for his nonviolent efforts to bring about change in the dehumanizing laws of South Africa. One of his most courageous campaigns was his protest against the pass laws in 1952, during which he burned his pass card and urged others to do the same. Luthuli's efforts were cut short, however, in 1959 when government officials took advantage of a law that allows them to "ban" an individual whom they feel is dangerous to the government. Without any trial or formal charges, Luthuli was

...the more blacks will turn to violence as the only solution.

placed under virtual house arrest. He was forbidden to attend any meetings or to leave his home, although he was allowed to travel to Norway to accept his Nobel award in 1960. Tucked away in a rural mission station, Luthuli was largely ignored until his death in 1967.

Tutu may be harder to silence. The government that sent Chief Luthuli into obscurity hasn't been able to prevent Tutu's influence from increasing. In 1984, he was named the Anglican bishop of Johannesburg, South Africa's largest city. Just two years later in 1986, Tutu became the first black Anglican archbishop in South Africa.

With unrest increasingly bubbling over into violence, and with more than 1,000 people killed in 1985 alone in confrontations with police and in strife among rival ethnic groups, a calming voice such as Tutu's is desperately needed. The little man in the familiar purple robe has strode through riot-torn townships to offer his help. While sternly warning of the violence that will come if apartheid is not abolished, Tutu has continued to stem violence where he can. More than once he has shielded a person from an attacking mob with his own body, and in one potentially deadly incident, he calmly worked out a compromise that defused a confrontation between police officers and a bitter crowd attending a funeral.

Archbishop Tutu's advice to concerned outsiders is to pray, to inform themselves, to put pressure on every international institution connected with South Africa, and to recognize injustice in their own societies. To Desmond Tutu, these measures represent the only hope of realizing peace. The price of ignoring his arguments has already been seen in the growing numbers of young South African blacks whose patience with the message of nonviolence is wearing thin. Yet Desmond Tutu clings to the hope that one day he, an internationally respected man who has inspired many with his words and actions of peace, may be allowed to vote in his own country.

Glossary

amnesty (AM-nes-tee) — forgiveness granted by a government for crimes, real or perceived, committed against it

apartheid (ah-PAR-tate) — the South African government's policy of segregation of racial groups and discrimination against nonwhites

boycott — the act of refusing as a group to use a service or product until certain conditions are met

civil rights — basic rights guaranteed to a person by law

diplomacy — the practice of conducting negotiations between nations

disarmament — the reduction or elimination of weapons and armed forces

dissident — a person who publicly disagrees with the official government position

divestment — the process of disposing of certain investments

economic sanctions — measures taken by one nation to hurt the economy of another nation

homelands — the 10 areas the South African government has set aside for the relocation of the different ethnic groups of black South Africans

manifesto (man-eh-FES-toh) — a public declaration of an opinion or an intention

martial law — the temporary control of a territory by the military when a disturbance makes the civilian government unable to enforce laws and maintain order

mediation — the act of intervening to solve differences between conflicting parties

militarism — the belief in using the force of the military to solve problems

nuclear fallout — the tiny radioactive particles that result from a nuclear explosion

paramilitary organization — a group separate from the military that is organized in a military fashion. Some paramilitary organizations work alongside military forces, while others work on their own.

pass laws — laws established by the South African government that call for all South Africans to have documents, or passes, that identify them by race. The laws limit the activities of certain racial groups, especially blacks.

poll tax — a tax of a fixed amount charged to all citizens, rich or poor. At one time in some parts of the United States, people who could not afford to pay the poll tax were not allowed to vote.

rearmament — the process of building up weapons and military forces after they have been reduced

segregation — the separation of a group from the rest of society, usually because of race

terrorism — the use of terror or intimidation, usually by a political group, to gain certain ends

totalitarian — related to a government based on the strict control of the lives of its people

Index

(Numbers in bold face refer to photographs)

ABOUT THE AUTHOR

Nathan Aaseng, who grew up in suburban Minneapolis, Minnesota, is a widely published author of books for young readers. He has explored far-ranging areas of interest, with college majors in English and biology, and work experience as a microbiologist/biochemist. Now a full-time writer, Aaseng has continued to delve into diverse subjects and has had more than 50 books published in the areas of sports strategy, biography, inspiration, and fiction. He now lives in Eau Claire, Wisconsin, with his wife and four children.

ACKNOWLEDGMENTS:
The photographs in this book are reproduced through the courtesy of: pp. 6, 22, 35, 40-41, National Archives; pp. 8, 9, 20, 49, 56, 65, 71, The Nobel Foundation; pp. 10, 13, Jane Addams Memorial Collection, University of Illinois at Chicago; p. 12, Swarthmore College Peace Collection; pp. 14, 15, 16, 18, 23, 24-25, Library of Congress; pp. 17, 47, 48, 62, Independent Picture Service; pp. 24 (left), 40 (left), 43, 44, 50, 57, 60, 64, 67, 68, 72, 75, UPI/Bettman Newsphotos; pp. 26-27, 33, Defense Nuclear Energy; pp. 28, 29, Los Alamos National Laboratory; p. 31, Oregon Historical Society; p. 36 (left), Schomburg Center for Research in Black Culture, The New York Public Library, Astor, Lenox, and Tilden Foundations; pp. 36-37, Birmingham Public Library, Birmingham, Alabama; pp. 39, 52, 55, 58, 74, Religious News Service. Back cover photograph courtesy of Jane Addams Memorial Collection, University of Illinois at Chicago. Cover art by Mark Wilken.